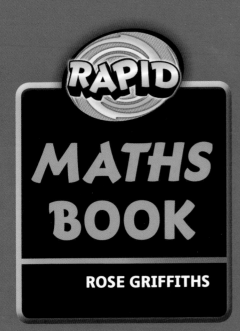

RAPID
MATHS BOOK

ROSE GRIFFITHS

Heinemann

Heinemann is an imprint of Pearson Education Limited, a company incorporated in England and Wales, having its registered office at Edinburgh Gate, Harlow, Essex, CM20 2JE. Registered company number: 872828

www.heinemann.co.uk

Heinemann is a registered trademark of Pearson Education Limited

Text © Rose Griffiths 1996, 2005, 2009

First published 1996
Second edition first published 2005
Third edition first published 2009

13 12
10 9 8 7 6 5 4 3

British Library Cataloguing in Publication Data
A catalogue record for this book is available from the British Library.

ISBN 978 0 435912 30 7

Designed and produced by Debbie Oatley @ room9design
Original illustrations © Pearson Education Ltd 2009
Illustrated by Pet Gotohda and Matt Buckley
Cover illustration © Pearson Education Ltd
Cover illustration by Pet Gotohda
Printed in China (CTPS/03)

Acknowledgements
We would like to thank Stapleford Abbotts Primary, Stapleford Abbotts and Queens Dyke Primary, Witney for their invaluable help in the development and trialling of this course.

The author and publisher would like to thank the following individuals and organisations for permission to reproduce photographs:

©Shutterstock / Losevsky Powell: p.8 and p.9 (button 1, 2 and 3); ©Shutterstock / Ana de Sousa: p.8 and 9 (button 4, 5, 6 and 7); ©Shutterstock / Losevsky Powell: p.9 (button 8 and 9); ©Shutterstock / Ana de Sousa: p.9 (button 10); ©Shutterstock / Mario Tarello: p.18 (calculator); ©Pearson Education / Tudor Photography: p. 30 (5 toy dinosaurs); ©Shutterstock / Lana Small: p. 31 (comb 1); ©Shutterstock / Stillfx: p.31 (comb 2); ©Shutterstock / Dole: p.31 (comb 3); ©Shutterstock / Claudio Baldini: p.31 (afro comb); ©Shutterstock / Losevsky Powell: p.31 (button 1, 2 and 3); ©Shutterstock / Ana de Sousa: p.31 (button 4 and 5); ©Shutterstock / Alena Yar: p.31 (3 pens); ©Shutterstock / Johanna Goodyear: p.43 (ball 1); ©Shutterstock / Perry Carrell: p.43 (ball 2); ©Shutterstock / Matthew Cole: p.43 (ball 3); ©Shutterstock / Mark William Parry: p.43 (ball 4); ©Shutterstock / Adrian Coroama: p.43 (ball 5); ©Shutterstock / Christopher Testi: p.43 (ball 6); ©Shutterstock / Celso Dupo: p.43 (ball 7); ©Shutterstock / Jip Fens: p.43 (ball 8); ©Shutterstock / Yuri Samsonov: p.43 (ball 9); ©Shutterstock / Alex Staroseltsev: p.43 (ball 10); ©Shutterstock / Dino O: p.43 (ball 11); ©Shutterstock / Kelpfish: p.43 (ball 12); ©Pearson Education / Tudor Photography: p.43 (3 toy dinosaurs).

All other photos © Pearson Education / Clark Wiseman, Studio 8.

Every effort has been made to contact copyright holders of material reproduced in this book. Any omissions will be rectified in subsequent printings if notice is given to the publishers.

Websites
The websites used in this book were correct and up-to-date at the time of publication. It is essential for tutors to preview each website before using it in class so as to ensure that the URL is still accurate, relevant and appropriate. We suggest that tutors bookmark useful websites and consider enabling students to access them through the school/college intranet.

Contents

Using this book

Your teacher will talk to you about where you will start in *Rapid Maths*.

Welcome to *Rapid Maths*.

Getting started

Check that you can do the first two pages in each part of this book, before you do any more.

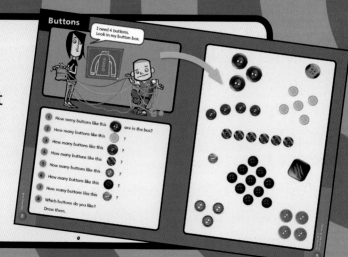

Reading

There are word lists in the Teacher's Guide.

These will help you learn any new words you need.

I've made cards from my list.

Extra activities

There are more activities and games in the Copymasters, Games Pack and Home Maths Book.

There is Practice Software too, with activities for each level of *Rapid Maths*.

Take them home for extra practice!

We do plenty of counting practice!

I think we've got more than 8 bricks here.

Progress tests and Record sheets

These are in the Teacher's Guide.

Check on your progress…

and keep a record of what you've done!

Part I
Contents

Counting and place value

Addition and subtraction

Buttons

1 How many buttons like this are in the box?

2 How many buttons like this ?

3 How many buttons like this ?

4 How many buttons like this ?

5 How many buttons like this ?

6 How many buttons like this ?

7 How many buttons like this ?

8 Which buttons do you like?

Draw them.

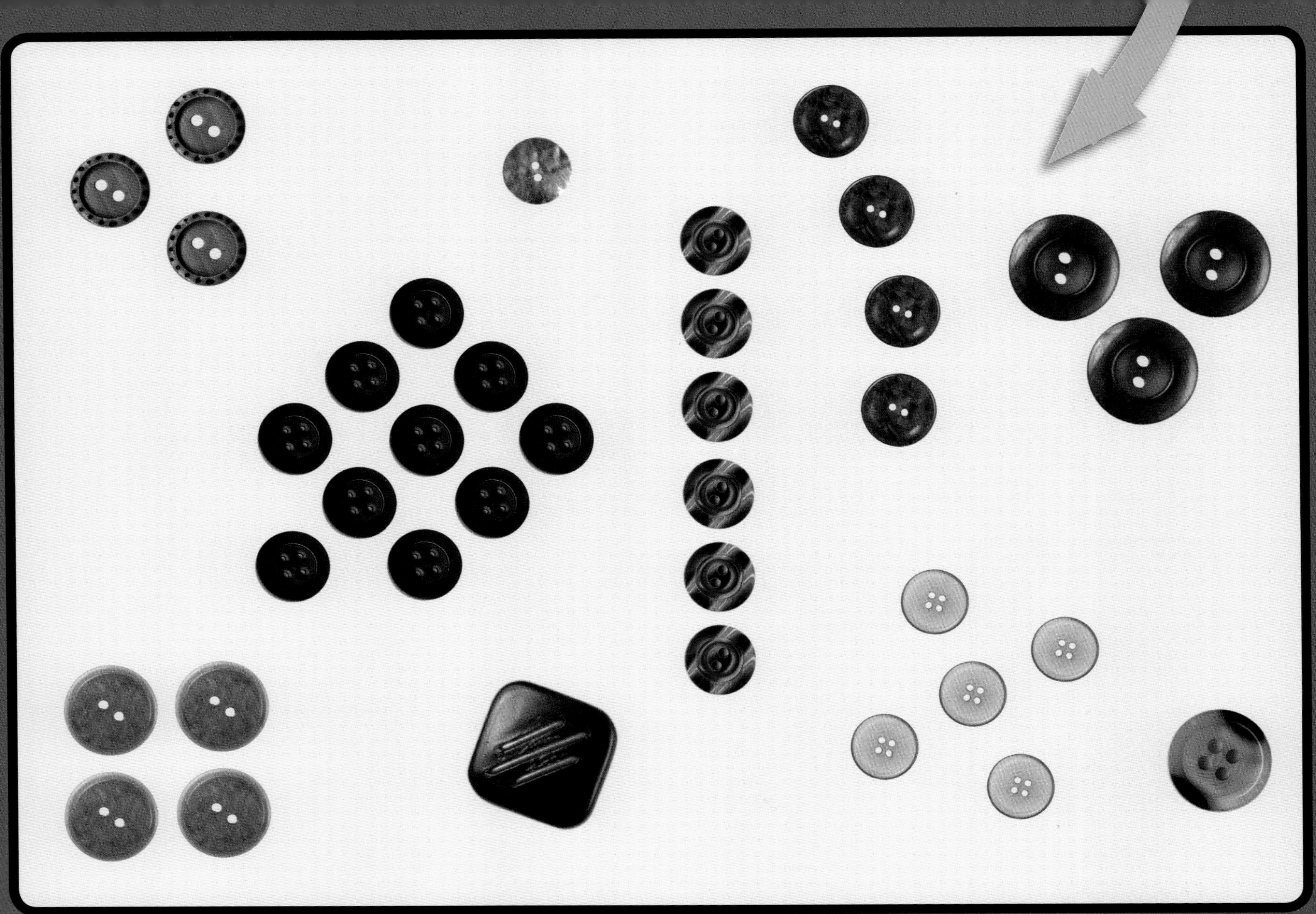

Neat numbers (1)

- Start by the dot.
- → Follow the arrows.
- 2 Nice smooth curve.
- 2 Straight bottom line.

- Start by the dot.
- → Follow the arrows.
- 2 Nice smooth curve.
- 3 Another smooth curve.

Go over the number with your fingers.

Start by the dot.

Follow the arrows.

— Straight top line.

7 Then the rest.

Go over the number with your fingers.

Write out these numbers neatly.

 222   333   222   333

 777   222   777   222

 333   777   333   777

 237   237   237   237

 723   723   723   723

Number lines

Here is a number line.

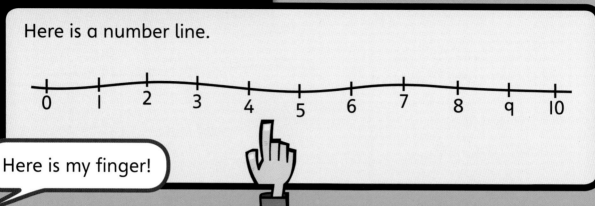

Here is my finger!

Which number is under my finger?

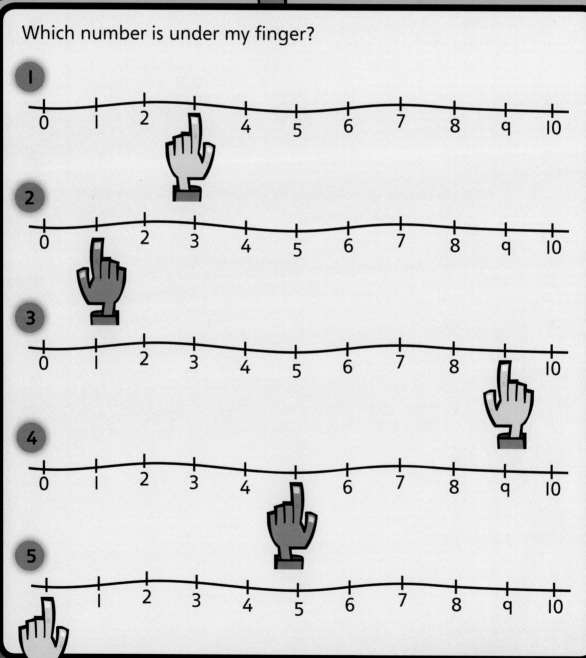

This number line goes backwards.

| | | | | | | | | | | | |
12 11 10 9 8 7 6 5 4 3 2 1 0

Which number is under my finger?

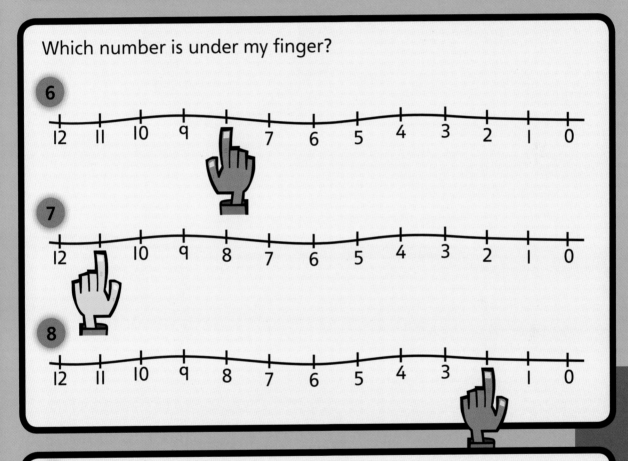

6

| | | | | | | | | | | | |
12 11 10 9 7 6 5 4 3 2 1 0

7

| | | | | | | | | | | | |
12 10 9 8 7 6 5 4 3 2 1 0

8

| | | | | | | | | | | | |
12 11 10 9 8 7 6 5 4 3 1 0

9

- Use the number lines at the top of these pages.
- Work with a partner.
- Take turns to ask: Which number is under my finger?

Go over the number with your fingers.

- Start by the dot.
- Follow the arrows.
- O One nice smooth curve.

Go over the number with your fingers.

- Start by the dot.
- Follow the arrows.
- o Smooth loop round.
- q Straight line down.

- Start by the dot.
← Follow the arrows.
S Smooth curves down.
8 Curve back to the top.

Go over the number with your fingers.

Write out these numbers neatly.

1	000	999	000	999
2	888	000	888	000
3	999	888	999	888
4	089	089	089	089
5	908	908	908	908

Counting cats

This cat is sad.   This cat is happy.

1 How many cats are sad?

2 How many cats are happy?

3 How many cats altogether?

4 How many cats are sad?

5 How many cats are happy?

6 How many cats altogether?

7 How many cats are sad?

8 How many cats are happy?

9 How many cats altogether?

10 How many cats are sad?

11 How many cats are happy?

12 How many cats altogether?

Ⓖ

Ask if you can play the 'Counting cats' game.

Counting to 10
Copymasters R9 and R10
The 'Counting cats' game (R29 and R30)

Calculators

This is my calculator.
Your calculator may be different.

display

add button

clear button

equals button

CASIO
SL-460L

1 Draw your calculator.

2 Use these words to label your drawing.

display   clear   add   equals

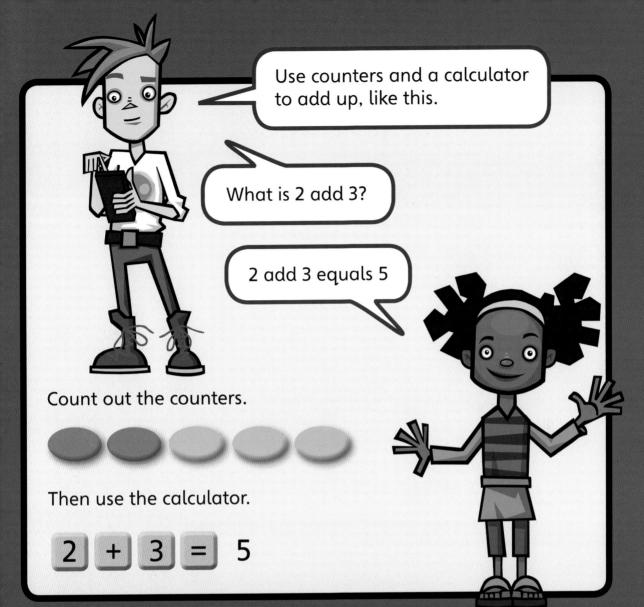

Use counters and a calculator to add up, like this.

What is 2 add 3?

2 add 3 equals 5

Count out the counters.

Then use the calculator.

2 + 3 = 5

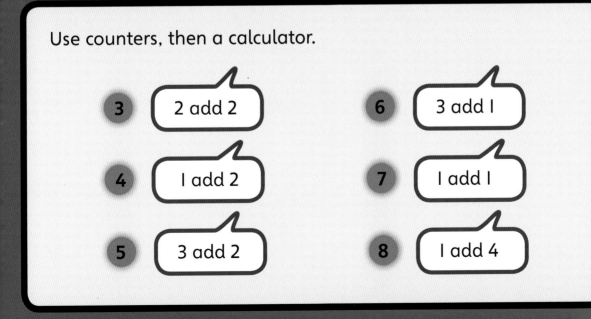

Use counters, then a calculator.

3. 2 add 2

4. 1 add 2

5. 3 add 2

6. 3 add 1

7. 1 add 1

8. 1 add 4

Neat numbers (3)

Go over the number with your fingers.

- ● Start by the dot.
- → Follow the arrows.
- ‒ Straight top line.
- 5 Then the rest.

Go over the number with your fingers.

- ● Start by the dot.
- ← Follow the arrows.
- 6 One nice smooth curve.

Now write out these numbers neatly.

1   555   666   555   666

2   565   565   565   565

All these sums add up to 5 _or_ 6.
Write out the answers neatly.

3 $4 + 1 =$

4 $2 + 4 =$

5 $0 + 5 =$

6 $3 + 2 =$

7 $1 + 4 =$

8 $4 + 2 =$

9 $3 + 3 =$

10 $6 + 0 =$

11 $2 + 3 =$

12 $5 + 1 =$

13 $1 + 5 =$

14 $0 + 6 =$

Cat sums

Count the cats.	Copy and complete.

5 sad cats   **No happy cats**

1   5 + 0 =

4 sad cats   **I happy cat**

2   4 + 1 =

3 sad cats   **2 happy cats**

3   3 + 2 =

2 sad cats   **3 happy cats**

4   2 + 3 =

Count the cats.

Copy and complete.

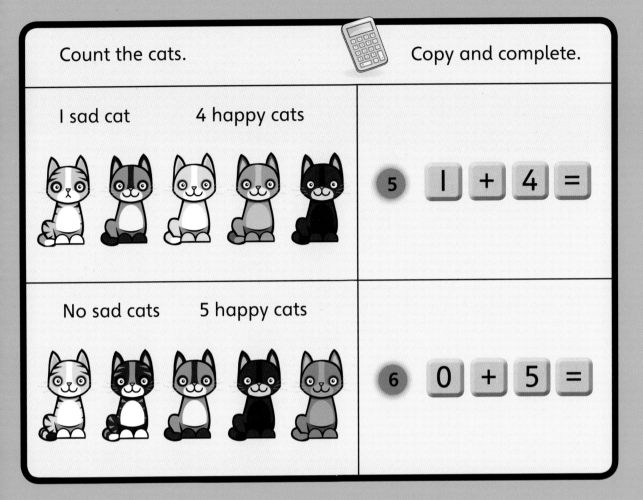

I sad cat   4 happy cats

5   1 + 4 =

No sad cats   5 happy cats

6   0 + 5 =

Ask if you can play the 'Make 5' game.

G

Addition bonds to 5
Copymasters R15 and R16
The 'Make 5' game (R31 and R32)

23

How many letters?

1 Write <u>your</u> first name.
How many letters are in your name?

How many letters are in these names?

2 **ADAM**

3 **MANJIT**

4 **LAURA**

5 **MIRIAM**

6 **ANDREW**

7 **CATHERINE**

LISA
AMY
JAMES
CHRISTOPHER
AARON
HIMESH
SAMANTHA
NEHAL
MATTHEW
KAYLEIGH

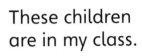

These children are in my class.

8 Which name is the shortest? How many letters?

9 Which name is the longest? How many letters?

10 Make a list of some children in your class.

How many letters are in each name?

Who has the shortest name?

Who has the longest name?

Rabbit hops

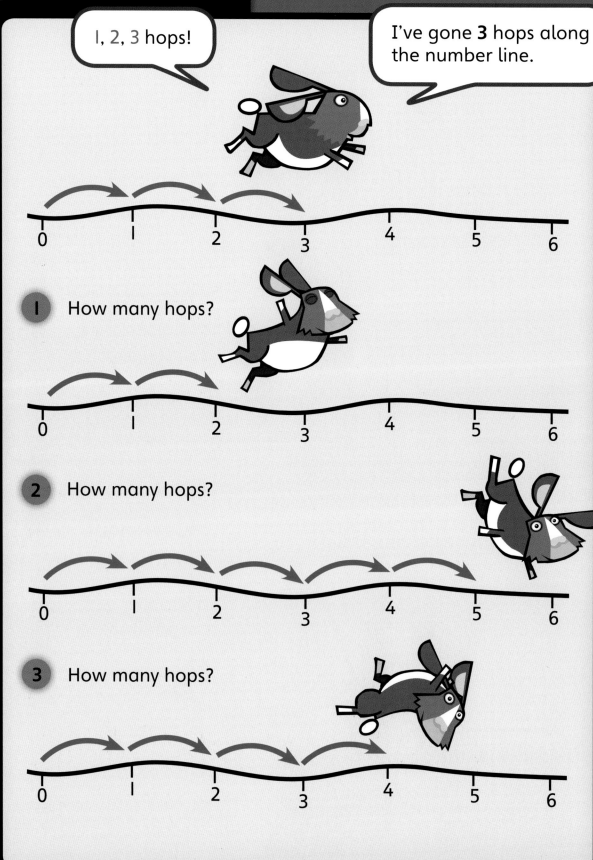

1, 2, 3 hops!

I've gone **3** hops along the number line.

1 How many hops?

2 How many hops?

3 How many hops?

2 hops then I hop...

That's **3** hops!

2 + I = 3

Count the hops.

Copy and complete.

3 hops then I hop.

4   3 + I =

4 hops then I hop.

5   4 + I =

5 hops then I hop.

6   5 + I =

I hop then 5 hops.

7   I + 5 =

Addition within 6
Copymasters R19 and R20

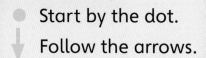

Go over the number with your fingers.

- Start by the dot.
- Follow the arrows.
- Down and across.
- Then down.

Go over the number with your fingers.

- Start by the dot.
- Follow the arrow.
- Straight line down.

Now write out these numbers neatly.

1 444   111   444   111

2 414   414   414   414

Remember:
Always start at the top when you write a number.

3 23   23   23   23

4 777   777

5 90   80   90   80

6 65   65   65   65

7 1 2 3 4 5 6 7 8 9 10

8 10 9 8 7 6 5 4 3 2 1

Taking away

Jo keeps taking things away!

---

4 cars … then Jo took 2 away.

1

2

How many are left?

4 − 2 =

↑

take away

---

5 dinosaurs … then Jo took 1 away.

3

4

How many are left?

5 − 1 =

---

3 books … then Jo took 2 away.

5

6

How many are left?

3 − 2 =

5 monsters ... then Jo took 3 away.

7
8

How many are left?

5 − 3 =

4 combs ... then Jo took I away.

9
10

How many are left?

4 − I =

5 buttons ... then Jo took 4 away.

11
12

How many are left?

5 − 4 =

3 pens ... then Jo took I away.

13
14

How many are left?

3 − I =

Sums in pairs

I hop, then 6 hops …that's **7** hops!

I + 6 = 7

Count the hops. Copy and complete.

6 hops then I hop.

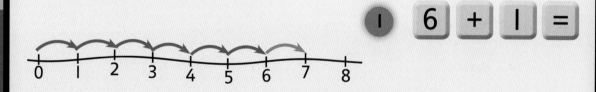

1 6 + I =

---

2 hops then 5 hops.

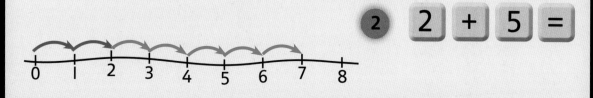

2 2 + 5 =

Count the hops. Copy and complete.

5 hops then 2 hops.

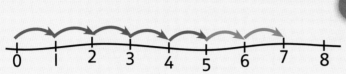

3 5 + 2 =

3 hops then 4 hops.

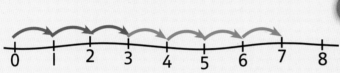

4 3 + 4 =

4 hops then 3 hops.

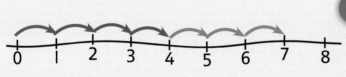

5 4 + 3 =

6 What is 5 + 2?

7 What is 2 + 5?

8 What is 7 + 0?

9 What is 0 + 7?

10 What is 3 + 4?

11 What is 4 + 3?

More taking away

What is 5 take away 2?

Count out 5 counters.

Then take away 2.

5

take away 2 ... leaves 3

Then use a calculator.

5 − 2 = 3

5 take away 2 is 3

Work with a partner.
Will you and your partner get the same answers?

1 7 take away 3

2 6 take away 4

3 4 take away 3

4 5 take away 1

5 7 take away 2

6 5 take away 3

7 6 take away 3

8 4 take away 2

Make 4

Does this make 4?

3 + 1

Does this make 4?

6 − 2

Does this make 4?

1 + 2 + 1

Yes! They all make 4.

There are lots of sums that make 4.
How many can you think of?
Write them down.

Ask a partner to check them.

Part 2
Contents

Counting and place value

Addition and subtraction

Multiplication and division

Counting

This baby is awake.   This baby is asleep.

1 How many babies are awake?

2 How many babies are asleep?

3 How many babies altogether?

4 How many babies are awake?

5 How many babies are asleep?

6 How many babies altogether?

7 How many babies are awake?

8 How many babies are asleep?

9 How many babies altogether?

10 How many babies are awake?

11 How many babies are asleep?

12 How many babies altogether?

13 How many babies are awake?

14 How many babies are asleep?

15 How many babies altogether?

Writing numbers

These numbers are messy.

Your 3 is back-to-front! You need to practise.

How to write numbers neatly.

Remember: Always <u>start at the top</u> when you write a number.

Look at these numbers.
Are they the right way round?
Write <u>Yes</u> or <u>No</u>.

1 **3**

2 **5**

3 **Ɛ**

4 **2**

5 **5**

6 **S**

7 **Ɛ**

8 **S**

Write out these numbers neatly.

9   123   123   123   123

10 455   455   455   455

11 68   68   68   68

12 Ask a partner to watch you.

Write 0 1 2 3 4 5 6 7 8 9.

Which numbers do <u>you</u> need to practise?

Toys

Put your toys away.

Look at the toys. ➡️

　　① 　How many balls?

　　② 　How many monsters?

　　③ 　How many cars?

　　④ 　How many dinosaurs?

Ask if you can play the 'Monsters in 3s' game.

Counting in groups of 3
Copymaster R36
The Monsters in 3s' game (R59 and R60)

Eight counters

You need 8 counters and a calculator.

4 add 2

Count out the counters.

Then use the calculator.

4 + 2 = 6

4 add 2 makes 6

Use counters, <u>then</u> a calculator.

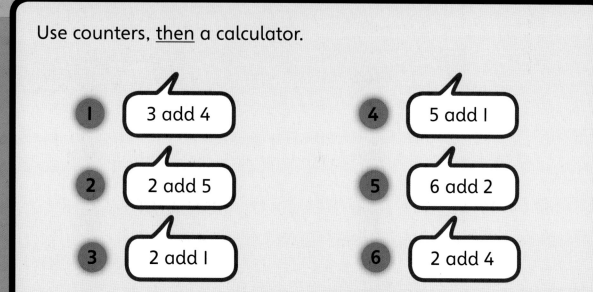

1. 3 add 4

2. 2 add 5

3. 2 add 1

4. 5 add 1

5. 6 add 2

6. 2 add 4

Use counters, <u>then</u> a calculator.

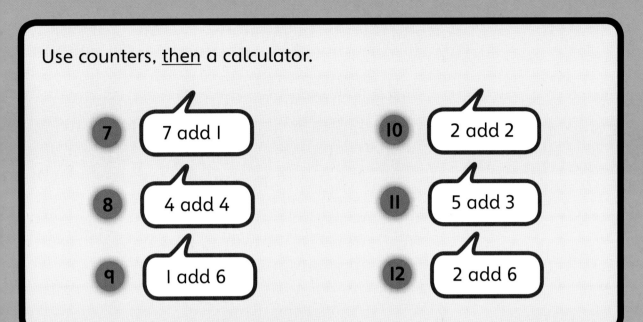

7 — 7 add 1

10 — 2 add 2

8 — 4 add 4

11 — 5 add 3

9 — 1 add 6

12 — 2 add 6

Are these sums right?
Write <u>Yes</u> or <u>No</u>.

13 — 2 add 3 makes 4

15 — 8 add 0 makes 8

14 — 1 add 5 makes 6

16 — 5 add 2 makes 7

Addition within 8
Copymasters R37 and R38

Stick pictures

You need 18 sticks and 2 buttons.

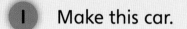

1 Make this car.

How many sticks did you need?

2 Make this dog.

How many sticks did you need?

3 Make this face.

How many sticks
did you need?

4 Make this face.

How many sticks
did you need?

5 Make this face.

How many sticks
did you need?

6 Make a face with
the sticks and buttons.

Draw it.

How many sticks
did you need?

Numbers in order

Here is a number line.

Here are some counters.

Which number is under each counter?

1

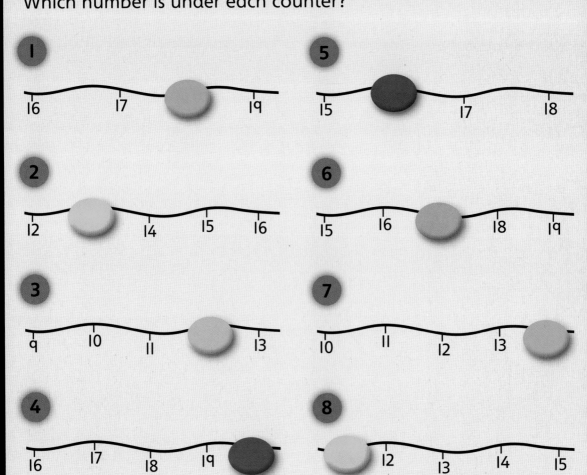

16   17   ___   19

5

15   ___   17   18

2

12   ___   14   15   16

6

15   16   ___   18   19

3

9   10   11   ___   13

7

10   11   12   13   ___

4

16   17   18   19   ___

8

___   12   13   14   15

Missing numbers

A game for two people. You need cards numbered from 0 to 20.

I'll shuffle the cards… then you take one. Don't let me see it!

Which card have you taken? I'll put the cards in order, to find out.

0 1 2 3 4 5 6 7 8 9 10 11 12 13 14 15 17 18 19 20

You've taken

16

16

Yes.
Now it's my turn to shuffle.

You can play several times.

Rabbit sums

This rabbit is sleeping.

This rabbit is hopping.

Count the rabbits.		Copy and complete.
6 rabbits sleeping  	No rabbits hopping	① 6 + 0 =
5 rabbits sleeping  	1 rabbit hopping	② 5 + 1 =
4 rabbits sleeping  	2 rabbits hopping 	③ 4 + 2 =

Count the rabbits.

Copy and complete.

3 rabbits sleeping	3 rabbits hopping

4 3 + 3 =

2 rabbits sleeping 	4 rabbits hopping 

5 2 + 4 =

I rabbit sleeping	5 rabbits hopping 

6 I + 5 =

No rabbits sleeping	6 rabbits hopping 

7 0 + 6 =

Addition bonds to 6
Copymasters R43 and R44

51

Pencils

I've got 10 pencils in this pack.

I've got 2 pencils.

We've got 12 pencils altogether.

Count the pencils.

 Copy and complete.

1	**2**
3	**4**
5 	**6**
7 	**8**

2. $10 + 3 =$

4. $10 + 5 =$

6. $10 + 8 =$

8. $10 + 9 =$

How many pencils?

9	**10**	**11**

12	**13**

I've got 10 pencils in this pack.

I've got 10 pencils.

$$10 + 10 = 20$$

That's enough for another pack of 10.

How many pencils?

14	**15**

Rabbit's food

Rabbit keeps
eating things.

8 carrots …then rabbit ate 1.

1 How many are left?

2 8 − 1 =

take away

7 lettuces …then rabbit ate 2.

3 How many are left?

4 7 − 2 =

7 carrots …then rabbit ate 3.

5 How many are left?

6 7 − 3 =

 3 cars ...I don't eat cars!

 **7** How many are left?

8 $3 - 0 =$

 4 carrots ...then rabbit ate 4.

9 How many are left?

10 $4 - 4 =$

5 lettuces ...then rabbit ate 3.

11 How many are left?

12 $5 - 3 =$

I'm full!

Counting in twos

How many bricks are here?

I can count them in ones...

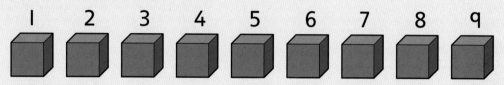

1 2 3 4 5 6 7 8 9

or in twos.

2 4 6 8 9

Count the bricks.

1 How many?

2 How many?

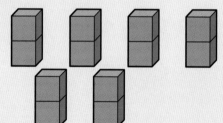

3 How many?

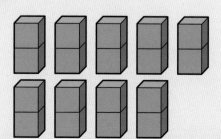

4 How many?

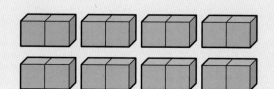

I'm counting in <u>ones</u>.
1, 2, 3, 4, 5, 6, 7, 8, 9, 10, 11, …

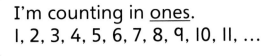

I'm counting in <u>twos</u>.
2, 4, 6, 8, 10, 12, 14, 16, 18, 20, …

5   2, 4, 6, 8, … What is the next number?

6   2, 4, 6, 8, 10, 12, … What is the next number?

7   2, 4, 6, 8, 10, … What is the next number?

8   2, 4, 6, 8, 10, 12, 14, 16, … What is the next number?

9   2, 4, 6, 8, 10, 12, 14, … What is the next number?

10   12, 10, 8, 6, 4, … What is the next number?

Fingers

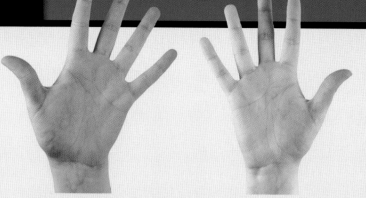

Fingers are good for sums up to 10.

Adding

4 + 3	= 7

Copy and complete.

1	6 + 2		6	2 + 5
2	1 + 4		7	3 + 4
3	5 + 5		8	8 + 1
4	7 + 2		9	2 + 1
5	3 + 3		10	6 + 0

Taking away

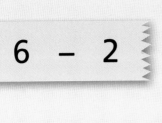

6 – 2

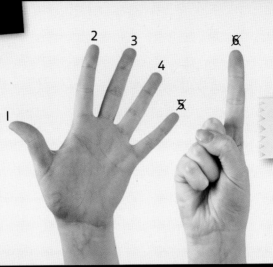

= 4

Copy and complete.

11	5 – 1		**16**	8 – 6
12	7 – 4		**17**	10 – 1
13	10 – 2		**18**	6 – 6
14	9 – 4		**19**	8 – 4
15	4 – 1		**20**	7 – 6

Check your answers. ✔ or ✗
How many did you get right out of 20?

Ask if you can play the 'Add or take away' game.

Addition and subtraction within 10
Copymasters R51 and R52
The 'Add or take away game' (R61 and R62)
Ⓖ

Sharing fish

6 fish shared between 2.

3 fish each.

None left over.

Share these fish between 2.

1 How many fish each?

2 Is there one left over?

Sharing between 2 within 12

60

Share these fish between 2.

3 How many fish each?

4 Is there one left over?

Share these fish between 2.

5 How many fish each?

6 Is there one left over?

Share these fish between 2.

7 How many fish each?

8 Is there one left over?

Share these fish between 2.

9 How many fish each?

10 Is there one left over?

Bouncing

3 bounces...

then 4 bounces.

How many bounces altogether?

$$3 \quad + \quad 4$$

7 bounces altogether

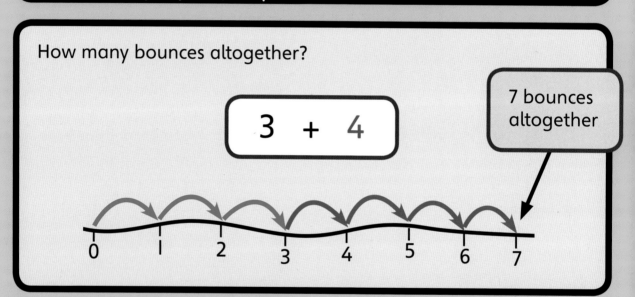

How many bounces altogether?

1	5 + 3	3	5 + 5	5	4 + 7
2	9 + 2	4	1 + 5	6	6 + 6

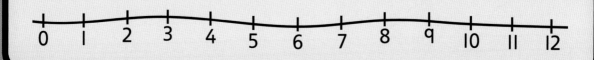

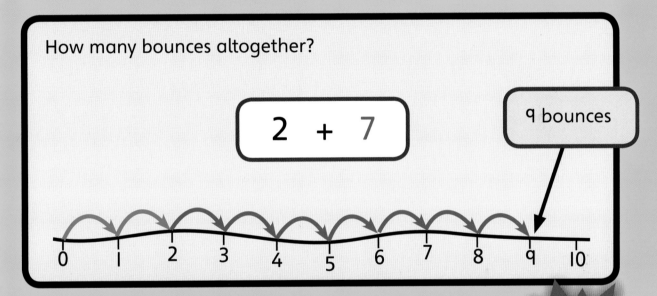

I'm bouncing, too.

2 bounces...

then 7 bounces.

How many bounces altogether?

2 + 7

9 bounces

0 1 2 3 4 5 6 7 8 9 10

Check

How many bounces altogether?
Use the number line on page 62.

 7   4 + 6   8   3 + 7   13   8 + 4

8   9 + 3   11   8 + 0   14   6 + 3

9   2 + 8   12   5 + 6   15   8 + 3

Addition within 12
Copymasters R55 and R56

Threes

The rabbits want 3 carrots each.

1 How many carrots altogether?

2  3 + 3 =

3 carrots each

3 How many carrots altogether?

4  3 + 3 + 3 =

3 carrots each

5 How many carrots altogether?

6  3 + 3 + 3 + 3 =

3 carrots each

7 How many carrots?

8 How many rabbits can have 3 each?

9 How many carrots?

10 How many rabbits can have 3 each?

11 How many carrots?

12 How many rabbits can have 3 each?

13 How many carrots?

14 How many rabbits can have 3 each?

I'll read these questions to you.
Do them in your head.
Write out the answers neatly.

1	4 + 1	5	1 + 1	9	2 + 4
2	3 − 1	6	2 + 0	10	6 − 4
3	2 + 3	7	6 − 1		
4	5 − 2	8	2 + 2		

I'll read you the answers. ✔ or ✘

1	5	5	2	9	6
2	2	6	2	10	2
3	5	7	5		
4	3	8	4		

Now I'll read these questions to you.

1	3 + 3	5	4 − 2	9	6 − 0
2	5 − 1	6	2 + 4	10	1 + 3
3	4 + 1	7	4 − 4		
4	2 + 2	8	1 + 1		

I'll read you the answers. ✔ or ✘

1	6	5	2	9	6
2	4	6	6	10	4
3	5	7	0		
4	4	8	2		

Make up some more questions to ask each other.

Part 3
Contents

Counting and place value

Addition and subtraction

Multiplication and division

Collections

I collect cats. I have 19.

1 Are they all here?

Phone numbers

Here is my phone number.

210 4361

Do you mean
270 4361
or
210 4301?

1 Copy these.

1	**2**	**3**	**4**	**5**
one	two	three	four	five

Write these.

2 Four two one,
two five two five

3 Three one two,
five two three four

4 Five four five,
one two three four

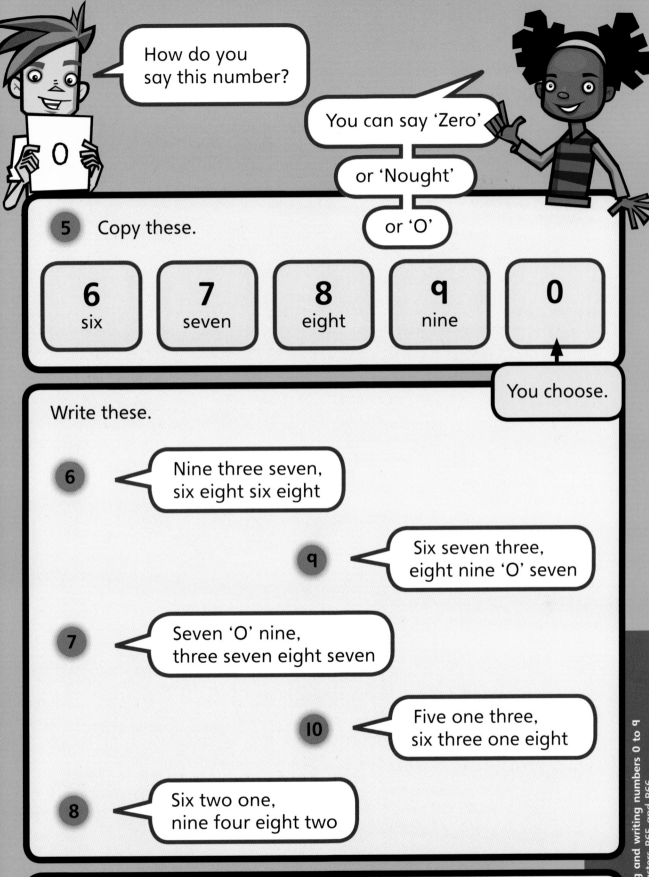

How do you say this number?

0

You can say 'Zero'

or 'Nought'

or 'O'

5 Copy these.

6	**7**	**8**	**q**	**0**
six	seven	eight	nine	

You choose.

Write these.

6 Nine three seven, six eight six eight

q Six seven three, eight nine 'O' seven

7 Seven 'O' nine, three seven eight seven

10 Five one three, six three one eight

8 Six two one, nine four eight two

Ask if you can play 'One to nine bingo'.

Reading and writing numbers 0 to q
Copymasters R65 and R66
'One to nine bingo' (R89 and R90)

Animal models

You need bricks.

1 Make this snake.

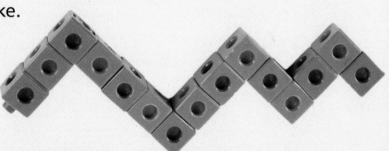

How many bricks did you need?

2 Make this snake.

How many bricks did you need?

3 Make this turtle.

Here it is upside down!

How many bricks did you need?

4 Make this fish.

How many bricks did you need?

5 Make this fish.

How many bricks did you need?

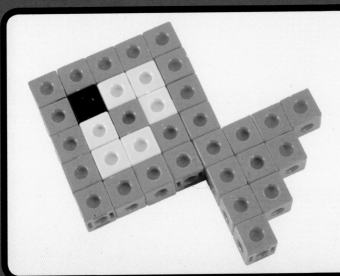

6 Make this frog.

How many bricks did you need?

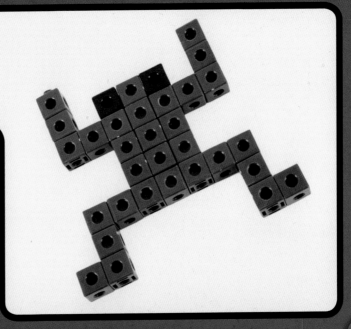

7 Make an animal.

How many bricks did you need?

Draw it neatly.

Turtle sums

Count the turtles.

Copy and complete.

7 turtles swimming	No turtles on the rock

1 7 + 0 =

6 swimming	1 on the rock

2 6 + 1 =

5 swimming	2 on the rock

3 5 + 2 =

4 swimming	3 on the rock

4 4 + 3 =

Count the turtles.

Copy and complete.

3 turtles swimming

4 turtles on the rock

5   3 + 4 =

2 swimming

5 on the rock

6   2 + 5 =

I swimming

6 on the rock

7   I + 6 =

No turtles swimming

7 on the rock

8   0 + 7 =

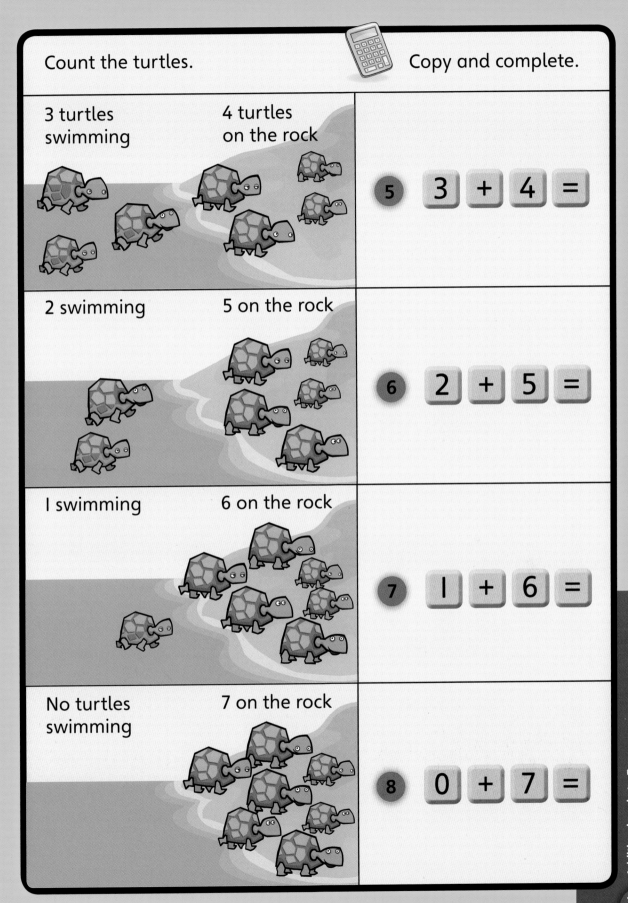

Make 10

There are 10 bricks here.

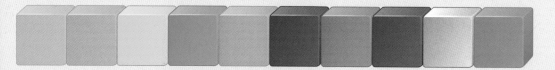

How many more bricks, to make 10?

 1

2

3

4

5

6

7

Make 10

A game for 2 people.
You need a calculator.

If I press

4 +

What will you press,
to make 10?

I'll press

6 =

Yes!

4 + 6 = 10

Now you play.
Have 6 turns each.

Use one of these numbers
to start each time.

1 2 3 4 5 6 7 8 9

Twos and ones

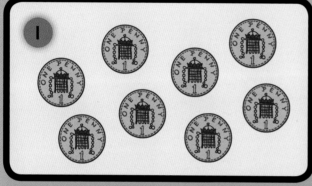

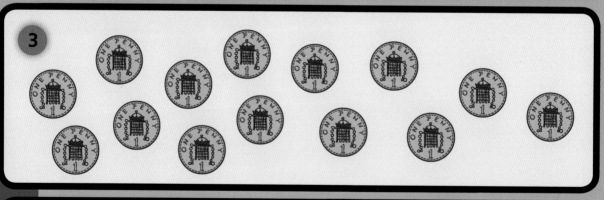

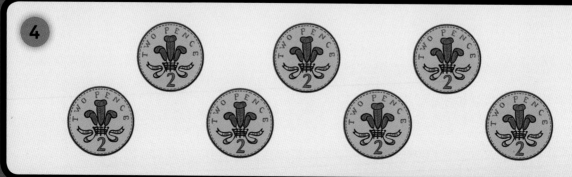

How much money is in each box?

5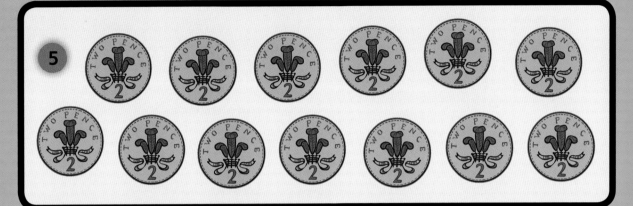

6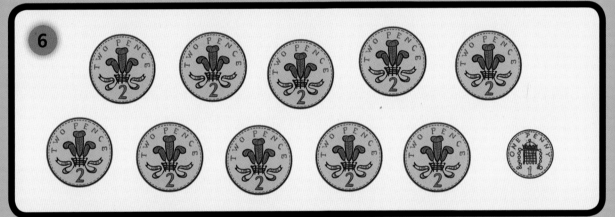

Make 12p with 2p coins and 1p coins.
There are lots of ways to do this.
Draw as many ways as you can.

This is one way.

Ask if you can play the
'Thirty pence' game.

Counting in 2s to 30
Copymaster R73
The 'Thirty pence' game (R91 and R92)

Rabbit and Frog

I hop one at a time.

Which number will I hop on next?

1

3

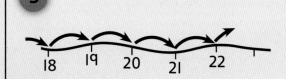

2

4

Rabbit can add one.

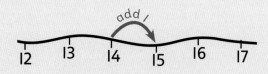

add 1

14 + 1

5 14 + 1 =

Rabbit can take away one.

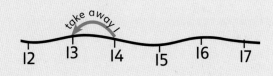

take away 1

14 – 1

6 14 – 1 =

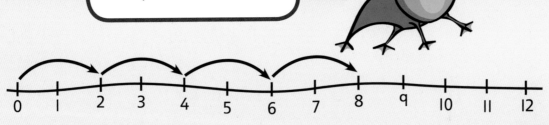

I hop two at a time.

Which number will I hop on next?

7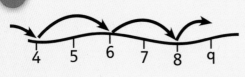

9

8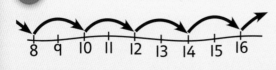

10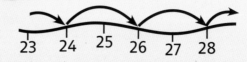

Frog can add two.

add 2

11 $14 + 2 =$

Frog can take away two.

take away 2

12 $14 - 2 =$

Pounds

Go over the number with your fingers.

- ● Start by the dot.
- → Follow the arrows.
- ℒ Nice smooth curves.
- — One short line.

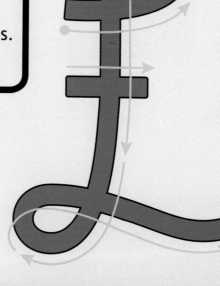

Practise writing
ℒℒℒℒℒℒ
then draw the line.
£££££££

1 Write these neatly.

ℒℒℒ ℒℒℒ ℒℒℒ

2 Now draw the line on each.

£££ £££ £££

How much money is here?   £5

How much money is in each box?

3

7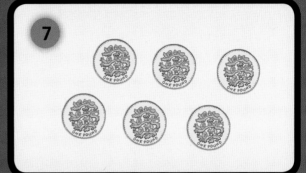

4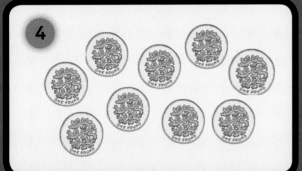

8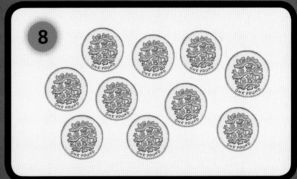

5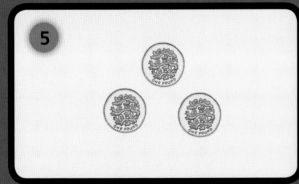

q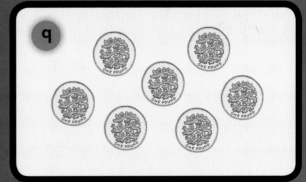

6

10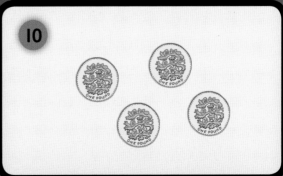

More pounds

This is £10 ...

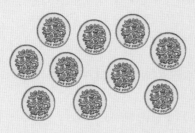

and this is £10.

How much money is in each box?

1

2

3

4

Work with a partner. Make 6 '£10 notes'.
Then play the game on page 85.

Count your money

A game for 2 people.
You need 6 '£10 notes',
30 '£1 coins',
a dice and a pot to
put the money in.

Throw the dice.
Look at the number you got.
Take that number of
pounds from the pot.

£3

Now it's your
partner's go.

After each go, count your money.
You can swap for a

The first person to get **£35** is the winner.

Frog hops

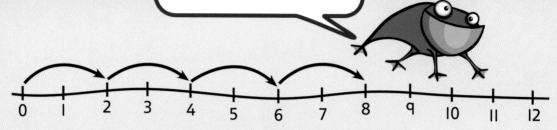

When Frog starts at 0, she hops onto 2, 4, 6, 8, …
0, 2, 4, 6 and 8 are <u>even</u> numbers.

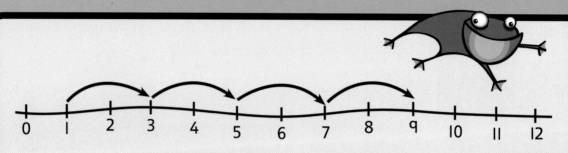

When Frog starts at 1, she hops onto 3, 5, 7, 9, …
1, 3, 5, 7 and 9 are <u>odd</u> numbers.

Which odd number will I hop on next?

1

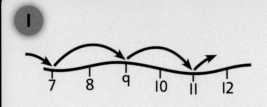

7 8 9 10 11 12

3

13 14 15 16 17 18

2

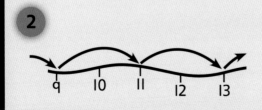

9 10 11 12 13

4

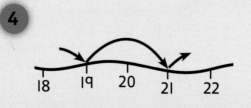

18 19 20 21 22

The even numbers are blue.

The odd numbers are red.

5   Start with 0. Write down the even numbers.

6   Start with I. Write down the odd numbers.

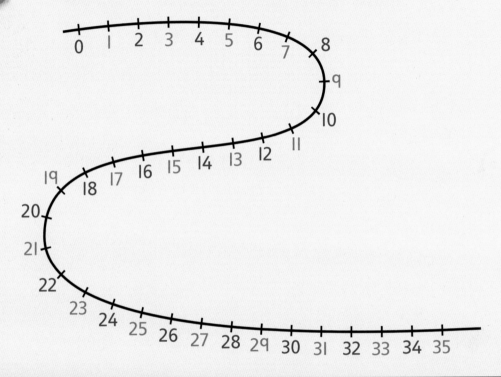

Write <u>even</u> or <u>odd</u> for each number.

7   8

9   15

11   20

13   29

8   3

10   18

12   23

14   32

Fives

How many tadpoles?

1

2

3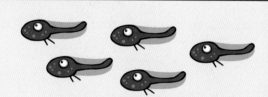

4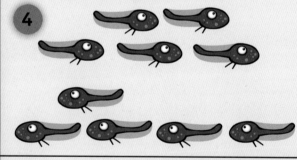

5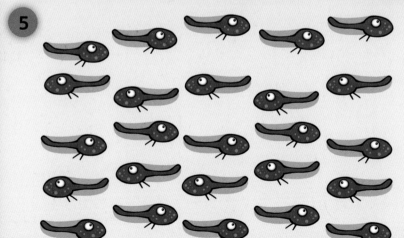

Multiples of 5 to 25

How many?

5

6 How many?

9 How many?

7 How many?

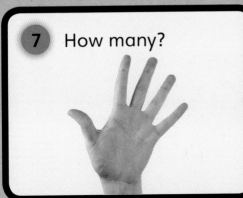

10 How many?

8 How many?

11 How many?

Centimetres

This is one centimetre. ——
This frog hopped 8 centimetres.

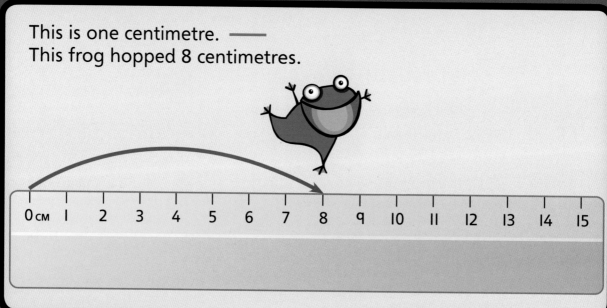

How far did the frogs hop? Use a ruler.

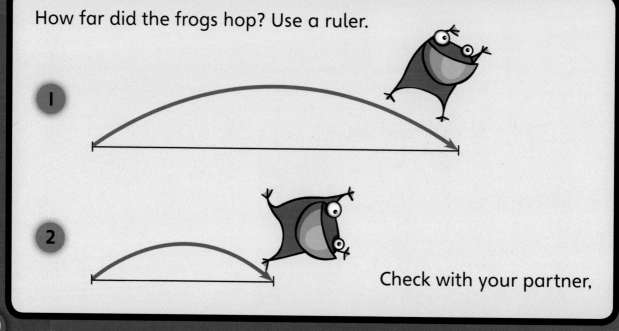

1

2

Check with your partner,

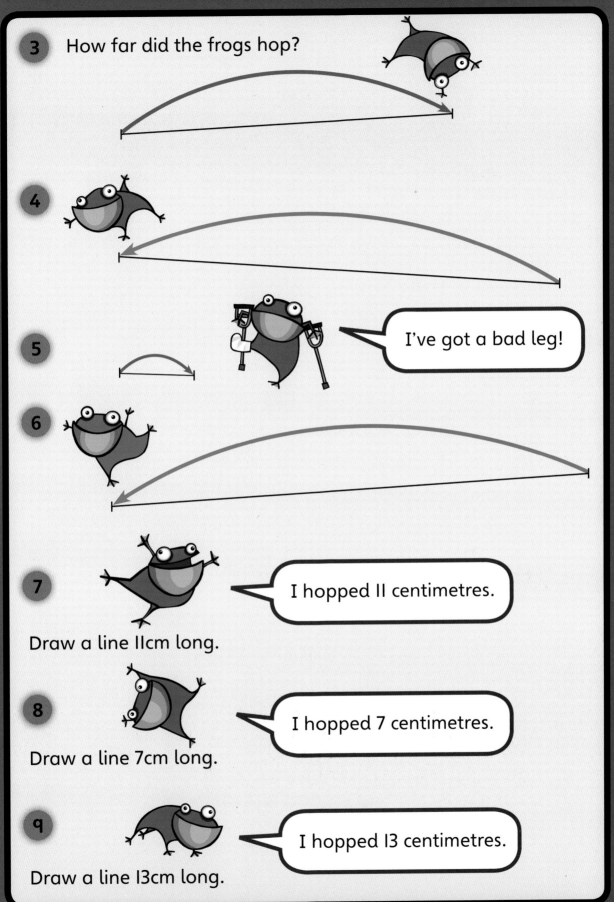

3   How far did the frogs hop?

4

5   I've got a bad leg!

6

7   I hopped 11 centimetres.

Draw a line 11cm long.

8   I hopped 7 centimetres.

Draw a line 7cm long.

q   I hopped 13 centimetres.

Draw a line 13cm long.

Rulers

I'm adding.

5 + 7

You can use a ruler to add or take away. It's like a number line.

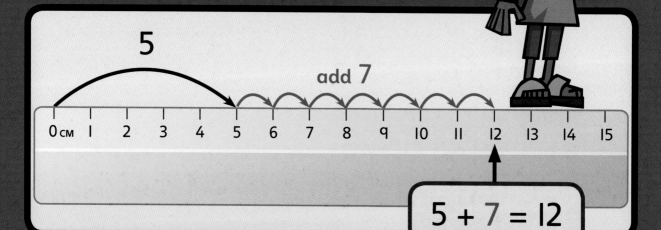

5

add 7

| 0 cm | 1 | 2 | 3 | 4 | 5 | 6 | 7 | 8 | 9 | 10 | 11 | 12 | 13 | 14 | 15 |

5 + 7 = 12

Use a ruler.

1	4 + 7	5	8 + 2	9	6 + 5
2	9 + 3	6	7 + 7	10	8 + 5
3	5 + 4	7	9 + 6	11	9 + 5
4	6 + 7	8	7 + 6	12	6 + 6

I'm taking away.

14 – 3

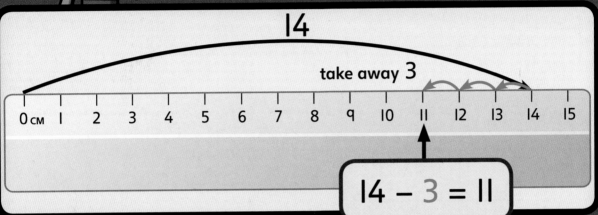

14

take away 3

| 0 см | 1 | 2 | 3 | 4 | 5 | 6 | 7 | 8 | 9 | 10 | 11 | 12 | 13 | 14 | 15 |

14 – 3 = 11

Use a ruler.

13	10 – 3	17	8 – 1	21	15 – 2
14	15 – 6	18	11 – 4	22	9 – 4
15	13 – 5	19	12 – 3	23	13 – 4
16	14 – 2	20	14 – 4	24	14 – 1

Now try these.

25	9 + 4	27	7 + 5	29	8 + 6
26	12 – 4	28	13 – 5	30	11 – 3

Mutliples of 5 to 25

Mutiples of 5 to 25
Copymasters R87 and R88

Does this make 7?

2 + 5

Does this make 7?

13 − 6

Does this make 7?

4 + 2 + 1

Yes! They _all_ make 7.

There are lots of sums that make 7.
How many can you think of?
Write them down.

Ask a partner to check them.